Positive Thinking
Change Your Thinking And Change Your Life

Ralph Sey

Table of Contents

INTRODUCTION

Positive thinking is widely defined as a technique that helps keep your thoughts optimistic and steer you towards positive outcomes. It does not relate to the pleasant, warm thoughts that flow through our mind when we are in a good mood and should not be confused with being generally happy—in fact, more often it can be when faced with adversity or unfortunate life events that the process of positive thinking is most important. Let's take the infamous Apollo 13 story as an example:

> In 1970, Apollo 13 was launched with the intention of landing on the moon. However, due to an explosion and many technical issues, they weren't able to fulfil their objective. For the crew on board and the team on the ground, the mission now became one of abject survival. Under extreme pressure, as well as the eyes of the world below upon them, the team kept calm and were able to come up with ingenious solutions to their perilous situation in order to safely return to Earth.

> As the crew member Jim Lovell later said: **" I was faced with a problem, and so, if I did nothing but bounce off the wall for 10 minutes, I would be right back to where the problem was."** They had to apply problem solving and not become consumed with fear or negative outcomes. In the words of fellow crew member Gene Kranz, **"You only worry about those things you can do something about."**

The Apollo 13 mission has become seen as a "successful failure" and a parable for the power of positive thinking.

Leading psychologists in the field of positive psychology, such as Martin Seligman, have shown that by changing how you think, you can change your life. Why does thinking have such a powerful effect? Well, our thoughts change how we feel, which in turn changes how we behave. It all starts with our thinking!

Positive thinking can:

- Increase overall happiness

- Reduce anxiety

- Improve performance at work

- Sustain motivation

As well as being an extremely powerful predictor of many life outcomes, such as a longer life span and being happier and more productive, it is also widely found that positive thinking can have an amazing effect on health by reducing stress. Stress, as many people know, can have a hugely detrimental effect on our bodies and physical condition. And the healthier we are, the less negative we can feel, and with better health, there may be fewer obstacles to climb.

LEARNING TO BE OPTIMISTIC

Positive thinking is a skill that may come naturally to some and may have to be learned and worked on for others. Seligman coined the term "learned optimism", meaning that having a positive outlook needs to be cultivated, even if you are already disposed to be a positive-minded person. For everyone, optimism has to prevail over pessimism, and we need to have an inner dialogue to keep negative thoughts at bay.

Perhaps the most important thing to understand about positive thinking—or any thinking for that matter—is that our thoughts drive our feelings and actions and not the other way around. As humans, we have the luxury of creating our own reality through the type of thinking we engage in and the emerging belief system and actions which result from these thoughts. Let's examine how this chain reaction works.

An optimist is someone who engages in positive thinking, and the result is a belief in good outcomes. This belief drives the kinds of actions that will be needed to achieve the desired result. For example, you may think about how hard you've worked to qualify for your chosen profession and believe that this will inevitably result in rewarding work. This belief results in a well-orchestrated job search. Compare this to the negative thinking of the pessimist, who sub-consciously engages in self-sabotaging behaviour. You don't think you're capable of the job even though you're qualified so you ensure failure by ramping up your own anxiety, rehearsing failure in your mind and, as a result, reducing your confidence.

In both these cases, thinking led to a belief system and, therefore, a course of action in line with this belief. With this in mind, it is easy to imagine how positive thinking might not only improve health, but also has the power to influence success in all areas of life.

Research has shown that while optimism comes easier to some than to others, it can be learned by everyone as it focuses on what we *do* rather than who we *are*. This implies that having a good attitude can greatly affect your life and outcomes, such as health and happiness. Research by Carver in 1997 demonstrated that among a group who had experienced being diagnosed with breast cancer, those with optimistic personality types experienced less distress and were coping better than those who with pessimistic personality types.

This shows that even in adverse situations, positive self-talk can help you stay on track when the going gets tough. And although someone with a serious, chronic disease may not be able to change its progression, positive thinking will certainly help alter their perception of it, and in this way, improve the quality of their life. A powerful tool, then, this positive thinking—and although it has an inherited, genetic component, the good news is that it can be learned at any age!

AIMS OF THIS BOOK

This book aims to guide you through the 7 key steps towards building effective, powerful, and sustained positive thinking. We will look at how you can identify and challenge negative thinking, and apply mindfulness techniques to overcome and steer yourself through any potential traps a pessimistic mind can create. We will take a holistic view of positivity, exploiting yourself inside and out, as well as the world around you, as there are many deep and reciprocal connections that can influence your thinking and behaviour.

Rather than focus on all the theory behind positive thinking, we want to make this a practical guide that gives you the tools to implement functional optimism in every aspect of your life. Each chapter identifies key actions that you can study and try for yourself.

As we have considered already, positive thinking is something that can be learned, but it isn't always easy, particularly if you are someone who is naturally predisposed to be pessimistic. Understanding what positive thinking is and what it can do for you is only the beginning; knowing how to apply it and identify it inside your mind and in your interaction with the world around you is the key.

First, let's consider the connection between mind and body.

THE MIND-BODY CONNECTION

"To keep the body in good health is a duty...otherwise we shall not be able to keep our mind strong and clear."
- Buddha

The mind is in constant communication with the body and the way in which we think, feel, and act can have a profound effect on our physical well-being. Thankfully, this mind-body connection is well documented—it is critical to be able to test and measure psychological constructs, such as positive thinking in a scientific way. Without this, we would be unable to say anything definitive about cause and effect, and bestowing the virtues of positive thinking would be less than credible.

This means that we want to be able to be able to say that happy people are healthier *because they have a positive outlook*, otherwise it would be equally plausible to assume that they are simply happier *because they are in good health*.

HOW WE CONSTANTLY PREPARE FOR THE WORST

Modern scientific evidence of the mind-body connection started with a study of the fight-or-flight response. This reaction activates the sympathetic nervous system, resulting in a number of physiological changes as a person prepares to respond to a perceived threat by either fleeing the scene or staying to fight. In addition to increased heart rate and blood pressure, this acute stress response causes increased blood-glucose levels, an inability to focus, and the shutting down of digestive and immune systems.

While fight-or-flight is a necessary and useful response, it was designed to be used sparingly! It can take up to an hour for the body to settle back into a pre-threat state once the sympathetic nervous system has been engaged. Negative thinkers place themselves in a constant state of alert—through thought patterns characterized by worry and fear. Being stuck in a cycle of negativity compromises the body by keeping it in a breaking-down state.

It is important to notice that the body does not distinguish between real and imagined threats—it responds in the same way to both. This means that every time we imagine future conflict, or relive past conflict in our minds, we are experiencing it again physically. I'm sure you can imagine how exhausted and miserable you would feel if you had to actually relive your biggest life challenges every single day. Yet, this is exactly what is happening when we pull them up and go over them in our minds—and we do this more often than we realise.

The opposite of the fight-or-flight response, if there were one, would be the "rest and digest response". It can be triggered through a number of relaxation techniques and is routinely used in the treatment of stress disorders. This relaxation response triggers the parasympathetic nervous system, bringing the body back into a healthy, restful state. Not surprisingly, this is the state in which positive thinkers spend most of their time.

BE CAREFUL WHAT YOU FOCUS ON

One of the hallmarks of positive thinking is good coping strategies—the ability to focus on solutions rather than roadblocks and to act accordingly. Turns out, this has added health benefits. In his research, Michael F. Scheirer was able to demonstrate that there is a link not only between optimism and psychological well-being, but also between positive thinking and recovery from physical trauma and disease. Compare this to the inability to see solutions associated with negativity—this mind-set has been linked to an increased risk of heart attack.

To see how positive expectations impact health, we need look no further than the "placebo effect". This phenomenon occurs when a group of patients are unknowingly administered an inactive substance during a clinical trial—typically a saline solution or sugar pill—and they respond with a positive outcome simply because they believe it will work. We receive this same kind of reaction from children all the time when we place a bandage over a scratch to "make it better".

The opposite result can also be observed—you can think yourself sick as easily as you can think yourself well. Who among us doesn't know someone who develops every side-effect associated with a new medication simply from reading about them; and it is well known in medical schools that many medical students will come down with "intern's disease", manifesting the symptoms of every ailment in the book as the result of their relentless focus on illness.

1. TAKE CHARGE:
YOUR ABILITY TO CHANGE

One of the greatest dangers of negative thinking is developing a sense of hopelessness and lack of control, and nothing is more effective at keeping you stuck. In psychological terms, this defeatist attitude is known as "learned helplessness".

LEARNED HELPLESSNESS & MOTIVATION

The term "learned helplessness" was first coined by Martin Seligman in his work with animals. He observed that dogs who had been conditioned to believe that they couldn't escape an electric shock eventually gave up trying even if the possibility of avoidance existed.

People who are habitually negative in their thinking also learn how to behave helplessly. With the perception that they have no control over their circumstances, they begin to resist any opportunity for change and ,in turn, may experience fewer positive outcomes in their life. The truth is if you can change your mind, you can change your life, but you have to believe that it is possible.

A sense of helplessness often goes hand in hand with poor motivation. As much as you can learn to feel helpless, you can also teach yourself to be motivated. Being motivated doesn't necessarily mean getting up and being continually pro-active, it can also mean having the intention and belief that you can influence the course of your life by thinking positively and acting accordingly. Even holding the belief that you can challenge negative thinking is itself a form of motivation.

When you have established the motivation to think and live optimistically, you may wish to help yourself along by setting new challenges and performance goals (many of which we have outlined for you in Step 4: Mindfulness Techniques).

REWIRING THE BRAIN

The relatively new science of neuroplasticity has provided us with valuable insight into the power of positive thinking. The adult brain is very plastic, or malleable, and has the ability to reorganize itself.

Many of us are aware of the work done with stroke patients, to help them regain language and movement functions despite injury to those parts of the brain responsible for these activities. The science of neuroplasticity has shown that through the practice of new activities, it is possible to form new connections in the brain to do the work of damaged ones.

Neural pathways in the brain are wired in such a way that much of our thinking is involuntary. It is as if we go to either positive or negative thinking by default—after years of practice, the brain has forged connections which supports either positive or negative thinking.

The good news is, you **can** teach an old dog new tricks! If we are willing to change the way we think, we can re-wire our brains. This forming of new habits is what underpins Cognitive Behavioural Therapy (CBT), a mode of treatment that addresses disorders by altering faulty thinking and, as a consequence, behaviour.

Negative thinking can be switched out for positive, but disciplined practice will be required in order to form new habits.

Key Actions

Overcoming resignation is about regaining personal control, which, with a little patience and a lot of practice, is certainly possible.

Start by identifying a situation in which you feel you have no control and use this as a tool for change. Remember, awareness is always the first step when we are trying to change our thinking. A good choice would be a situation in which we find ourselves saying "yes" when we really feel "no".

Take note of the trigger(s) associated with the situation. Is it work related? Is it a way you typically respond around certain people?

Identify what you get out of the situation. Even negative behavior or thinking serves some purpose. Does it get you off the hook? Help you to avoid confrontation?

Then write a script for how you could have handled it differently. Remember that some level of personal control is available to us in every situation, and going through this exercise will help you see this.

Try the journaling techniques which can be found later in this book–these will help you to reframe negative thinking and to develop a focus on the positive.

Derive satisfaction from taking responsibility for your thinking–knowing that you are in control of the thought patterns which drive your reality is in itself a positive thought!

1. When difficult situations arise, look for the lesson in them. This is how we develop resilience in life–by learning what we can control in any given situation and focusing on that the next time around. "I will handle this differently next time" reads very differently from "That was just terrible."

2. Focus on the present–don't let negative thoughts gather steam by drawing on the past and projecting into the future. The mindfulness techniques which follow can help you with this.

3. Identify what you want, rather than thinking about what you don't want.

4. Engage in positive activities with positive people.

2. IDENTIFYING NEGATIVE THINKING

Negative thinking is a destructive habit that feeds upon itself. Something happens and we react badly to it, internalising the negativity and interpreting the events in a pessimistic way. Our thoughts surrounding this event drum up negative feelings, which drive more negative thoughts and actions. The only benefit associated with being caught up in this kind of cycle is that it may provide us with the imperative to change.

The effects of negative thinking are far reaching, and may include:

- Low self-esteem
- Feelings of powerlessness
- Higher incidence of depression and anxiety
- Less energy and reduced motivation
- Less success in all areas of life
- More physical complaints

There are some general characteristics associated with negative thinking, and being aware of the following will help you to assess your own.

1. Negative self-labelling: "I'm a fraud, if people really knew me, they wouldn't like me."

2. An unwillingness to see the positives: "Life is a big disappointment, everything is difficult. If things do work out, it's because I got lucky."

3. An excessive need for approval in order to feel just OK.

4. Mind reading: You think you know what others are thinking. For example, "She's just saying she like my hair because she wants me to look awful."

5. Dwelling on the negative in the belief that self-reflection will help find a way out.

Negative thinking may be centered in one of three areas:

1. Thoughts about self: Thoughts of not being good enough tend to be the most pervasive.

2. Thoughts about others: These center around blaming others for your unhappiness, making you the victim, and robbing you of a sense of control over the direction your life is taking.

3. Thoughts about the world: Pessimism leads to the general view that life is difficult and no one is really happy.

TYPES OF NEGATIVE THINKING

As early as the 1960's, psychiatrist Aaron Beck—long considered the father of Cognitive Behavioural Therapy—proposed that negative thinking is at the root of many disorders. By 1980 David Burns, a student of Beck's, had named and identified various kinds of negative thinking in his book entitled *Feeling Good: The New Mood Therapy*. Thanks to the work of these men, many kinds of negative thinking patterns have been given common names and are now known to us as "cognitive distortions". These give us a template from which to work when trying to assess our own thought patterns.

See if you recognize yourself in any of the following examples:

The Belief that Feelings Drive Behaviour

Waiting until you feel good about something before you take action, when taking action is actually what will make you feel good.

Example:

Waiting until you feel more energetic to start on an exercise regime, when exercising is what will give you more energy.

Filtering

A kind of tunnel vision which causes you to focus on an insignificant detail rather than seeing the whole picture.

Example:

You may have had a perfectly wonderful day–the weather was great, work went smoothly, you had dinner with an old friend–but your telephone bill for last month was higher than expected so, when asked, you say you had a terrible day.

Jumping to Conclusions

Thinking you know the reason why something has happened without doing a reality check.

Example:

You haven't heard back from a potential client when they said they'd call. Rather than getting in touch with them, you assume they are playing a waiting game to make you reconsider your offer.

Catastrophizing

Always expecting the worst possible outcome.

Example:

Getting through security at the airport is taking longer than you expected so, even though you've allowed yourself plenty of time, you're convinced that you're going to miss your flight.

Overgeneralization

Having a bad experience with something and assuming the result will be the same the next time. Alert: do "always" or "never" find their way into your vocabulary too often?

Example:

One rejection in a social or job situation translates into "Nobody likes me" or "I'll never get hired".

Polarized Thinking

No grey area—things or people are either good or bad.

Example: If I don't get straight A's, I'm a poor student.

Blaming

Believing that others are responsible for our feelings and problems.

Example:

Finding yourself saying "You're making me feel bad about myself", in response to something someone has said. People are entitled to say what they will; how you choose to think and feel about it is your responsibility.

Should's

A belief in unbending rules which apply to everyone.

Example:

People should return phone calls in a timely manner. If others don't, you feel angry; if you don't, you feel guilty.

Personalization

You are at the center of the universe and everything that happens is about you.

Example:

A co-worker's bad mood must be the result of something you did to irritate them.

Global Labelling

An overgeneralization paired with emotional labeling.

Example:

You missed one of your son's soccer games so you are a "terrible parent".

A Need to be Right

Your opinions or ideas have to be right in order for you to feel OK about yourself.

Example:

You need to win an argument at all costs, and you would rather be right than happy.

Control Fallacies

You either feel responsible for everyone else's happiness or a victim of external forces.

Example:

Your spouse is having a bad day and is feeling unhappy and you automatically assume it must be something you did.

You don't take responsibility—if you performed poorly at work it was because the job wasn't explained to you properly.

Fallacy of Fairness

If this expectation is not met, you feel bitter and angry.

Example:

Sorry folks, life isn't always fair. Someone may get the job or best seat in the restaurant just because they know someone.

<u>Reward Fallacy</u>

You believe in a direct connection between sacrifice and tangible rewards. Hard work can be reward in itself. There is not always an external pay-out.

Example:

You go above and beyond at work without being asked and are upset when you get a "well done" rather than a promotion.

Key Actions

Shining the spotlight of understanding on a problem is very often enough for the problem to go away. However, if you truly want to change your thinking in an effective way, keep a diary or write down the difficult challenges you face in as much detail as possible. Using the types of negative thinking outlined above as a template, identify the kind of distorted thinking you typically engage in. In this way, you may see how it was unconstructive and may also learn how to avoid it in the future.

Counsellors use this kind of methodology to help identify your problematic thinking patterns, so that they can help you to find the correct approach.

3. CHALLENGING NEGATIVE THINKING

"Do not wait to strike until the iron is hot;
but make it hot by striking."
– William B. Sprague

Positive thinking without action to back it up is what is commonly known as daydreaming! Thinking positively about that dream job is meaningless if you're not willing to back it up with the legwork: network, hand out CV's, upgrade your qualifications.

The hidden danger in not connecting positive thinking with action is the mistaken belief that negative outcomes are the result of being a bad person—which starts the whole cycle of negative thinking all over again.

Create a vision of what you want. Transform this vision into a plan that includes goals and deadlines. Commit to this vision by writing it down and by making your desires known to those around you. Visualization techniques are often employed by sports psychologists to help athletes reach their greatest potential. They are encouraged not only to imagine a successful outcome to their event or training session in as much detail as possible, but also to imagine how this feels. Repeated imagery and mental rehearsal, can be a great technique for anyone who wishes to alter their way of thinking—not only does it keep you focused on the positive, it can help instill confidence in your ability to succeed.

Above all else, do something, *anything*, to avoid staying stuck:

- Try solving an old problem with a new approach to get things started.

- Challenge your negative thoughts. For example, if you're constantly worried about losing your job, ask yourself—"If I lose my job, would my world really end?"

- Try grading your issues: assigning them a number between 1 and 10: 1 being terrible and 10 being good. See how much you currently exaggerate the impact of things—for example, very few things in life merit being rated as "terrible".

FIXED VERSUS GROWTH MINDSETS

As previously mentioned, Martin Seligman coined the term "learned optimism," which means that people can learn to be positive and that optimism is a skill that can be learned and cultivated. Like all skills, optimism may come more easily to some than others, but in theory it is something that everyone should have the facility to learn. However, your willingness to learn and to challenge negative thoughts may be strongly influenced by your overall type of thinking, or your "mindset".

Psychologist Carol Dweck spent two decades researching the idea of different mindsets and how they may influence intelligence and success. She identified two key mindset types with vastly different characteristics. The first type is what she called a "fixed" mindset, where someone believes that their basic abilities and talents are fixed traits. They believe that they are born with innate abilities and nothing will make much difference to their performance or level of success in life. In these types of people, failures are taken personally and are seen as showing up their inadequacies.

A "growth" mindset thrives on challenge and finds encouragement in failure. Those with a growth mindset are more likely to learn from criticism and enjoy engaging in effort and challenging themselves. They believe that they have the capacity to learn and change and do not accept that they are born with limitations.

Dweck found that each type of mindset led to directly associated thoughts and actions; in other words, the type of mindset had a profound effect on a person's thoughts and behaviour and can be seen as defining their life in general.

In this way, those with a growth mindset are more likely to be optimists, as they have the belief in change and the desire to challenge negativity and learn from mistakes. Those with a fixed mindsets are more likely to be pessimistic, internalising setbacks as showing up their lack of skills, and becoming defeatist at any attempt to change.

STRATEGIES

There are many different ways to challenge negative thinking, and you will have to find what works best for you. Whatever strategy you decide to start with, there a few things which should always underpin this process:

1. First, become aware of your negative thinking patterns. Your mindfulness practice will be a great help to you as you try to unearth these.

2. Assure yourself that you are in control—you get to decide what to dwell on. Personal control is dependent upon your attitude and not the situation at hand. Identify a difficult situation, try to see how it is specific—it does not involve or color everything in your life. Try to reframe it in a way which does not involve blaming yourself. Remind yourself that this situation is temporary—nothing remains the same forever.

3. Formulate a plan to replace the bad with the good—do this consciously and over time it will come more naturally.

4. Practice makes perfect—neuroplasticity is an amazing scientific discovery but to access its benefits will take a concerted effort. Keeping a journal or committing to a new course of action takes dedication and has to be done on a regular basis. Modern technology makes this a convenient process—notes for your journal can be kept on your phone or tablet throughout the course of the day—for work on when you have more time. A later section in this book will go into journaling in detail.

5. Be patient—change takes time. Once you get into the habit of positive thinking, a new cycle of creation will be at work. If practiced daily, it will take approximately 20 days before new behaviours become habits. There is a great free app called "Great Eastern 21 Days" which can help you in this regard—it allows you to earmark the behaviour which you wish to form into a habit, and doles out reminders to help you achieve this.

THE IMPORTANCE OF LANGUAGE

> Your beliefs become your thoughts,
> Your thoughts become your words,
> Your words become your actions,
> Your actions become your habits,
> Your habits become your values,
> Your values become your destiny.
> - Mahatma Ghandi

The subjective reality that we create for ourselves is expressed through language, regardless of whether it is verbalized or remains as an unspoken thought. Both our thinking and linguistic patterns tend to become routine over time—we get lazy with our language!

Your choice of words is important and can influence whether your thinking tends towards positivity or negativity, so choose them carefully. Consider the following:

1. Refer to your challenges as situations, rather than problems. To say "I have a difficult problem at home" is negative in tone compared to saying "I have a difficult situation at home". The word situation connotes something that is easily solvable.

2. Eliminate "always" and "never" from your vocabulary whenever possible, replacing them with "often" and "seldom". Very few things in life are as finite as "always" and "never", and they tend to exaggerate a situation—needlessly skewing it in a negative manner.

3. Switch "should have" with "could have". Telling yourself that you should have done something is a condemnation, whereas acknowledging that you could have done something different is reminding yourself that you have the ability to choose differently next time.

4. Start to think of and refer to "mistakes" as "valuable lessons". You will be much happier to think "There is a valuable lesson to be learned here", rather than the inference of failure attached to "I made a mistake".

5. As part of your inner dialogue, replace "must" with "prefer". Instead of telling yourself that you must complete your to-do list by Friday afternoon, try saying that you would prefer to get it done before the weekend. This will help pull you out of the realm of "all or nothing" thinking.

The best way to become sensitized to your choice of language is through writing—another great reason for keeping a detailed journal! If you have a willing friend, you could also record yourself talking to them about your challenges, in order to see how you describe them.

REFRAMING TECHNIQUES

There are also techniques for changing the way we *interpret* situations. These so-called "reframing" techniques help change the angle or context of something so that we can see it differently and help us respond in a more effective way.

Reframing techniques are diverse and there are many specific exercises that can help you adjust to any situation and create a positive attitude. Below we have outlined some of the key ideas.

Context reframing means that you can have the ability to simply convert a negative situation into a positive one by changing the *context* of how you understand it. It is a particularly useful way of quickly adapting to a sudden situation that is out of your control and can help you keep calm and remain productive, rather than focus on the negative event. For example, you miss the train on the way to work and decide to see it as an opportunity to read another chapter of the book that you are enjoying, rather than worry about having to explain being late to your boss.

A well-known model of reframing is the ABC Model proposed by clinical psychologist Albert Ellis, in which he explains how it is our interpretation of events that cause unhappiness, rather than the actual event. The basic model is as follows:

A—Activating event: something that happens around you. For example, your partner leaves you.

B—The belief that you gain from this event. For example, "I am unlovable".

C—Consequence: the emotional response to the belief. For example, "I will never enter a relationship again".

Ellis's fundamental idea is that people can think themselves out of distress and rationalise the situation, putting things in perspective. This helps give rise to healthier beliefs that encourage learning and finding positives in the interpretation of events.

BUILDING RESILIENCE AND THE A.P.E. TECHNIQUE

One essential aim of reframing your thoughts is to build *resilience* since a resilient person will be less worn down by a crisis or criticism and can enhance their capacity to remain positive in any situation. In the popular self-help book *The Resilience Factor*, psychologists Karen Reivich and Andrew Shatte analyzed decades of research to boil down the most important factors that affect and boost resilience, including avoiding thinking traps, detecting icebergs, challenging beliefs, putting it all in perspective, calming, and focusing.

In this way, *The Resilience Factor* took Seligman's work about learned optimism one step further by giving individuals the tools to teach themselves resilience (and through resilience, optimism).

In an online article, psychologist Senia Maymin was inspired by the book, and in particular, by the 3 main principles of getting out of a bad mood, as being in a bad mood can fill us with negativity and block us from being able to progress or learn. The three main principles are alternatives, perspective, and evidence, or A.P.E. Let's look at each of these 3 factors:

A—Alternatives. Moving forward from a bad mood can start with generating alternate beliefs. Quite often our bad moods make us believe that we are always at fault and that everything is going wrong. Just by correcting the emphasis and telling yourself that it is not always *your* fault, and it isn't *always* bad and that it's not *everything* that's a problem.

P—Perspective. Putting the situation that has led to the bad mood in perspective by visualising problems as an object and reducing it down to a small object makes it already feels much more manageable. Consider your life compared to others in the world: are you really having the worst day possible compared to other people? Encouraging flexibility in your thinking and being able to put problems in perspective means that you can minimize the impact of bad moods on your life, even if you can't always control what causes them.

E—Evidence. Try and find concrete evidence to the contrary of your bad mood. For example, if you are feeling like a failure because you have been rejected at a job interview, write down some examples of when you have succeeded in the past. Even small examples are enough to break down the wall that a bad mood can build up in your mind.

Finding your way out of a bad mood is essential to remaining positive and focused, and the A.P.E. method is a quick and easy-to-remember way to do just that.

NEURO-LINGUISTIC PROGRAMMING

Neuro-linguistic programming (NLP), a term which was coined by Dr Richard Bandler in the 1970s, is a method of training the brain through language and other forms of communication in order to reprogram the way the brain responds to various stimuli, such as people, events, and situations. NLP techniques aim to influence thoughts and behaviour long-term by making the brain gradually learn a certain response to the point that we are not consciously aware of it any longer. One of the most interesting NLP techniques is the 6-step reframing technique, which is relevant to positive thinking. The crux of the idea is that for each problem behaviour or thought process that there is a metaphorical "part" of your brain that is responsible and that you can communicate with and hope to influence. When referring to a problem, people often say "part of me wants to stop doing something, but another part of me wants to continue".

The six steps are as follows:

1. Identify the pattern of behaviour that is causing trouble and needs to be changed.

2. Establish a connection and communicate with the part causing the behaviour.

3. Try to understand what the part has been trying to do when it has been causing the certain behaviour, and try to discover the positive intention in that behaviour. If it is hard to ascertain, keep exploring until you have an answer.

4. Engage your creative part to generate alternate behaviours that will satisfy the intention identified above.

5. See if the part will accept the new behaviour and if it will identify triggers for this behaviour.

6. Ecological check, meaning that you see if the other parts disagree or are incongruent with the new behaviours you have introduced.

Although identifying the part involved and learning to identify the troublesome behaviours may take some practice, this approach can be helpful in the long-term re-wiring of negative or unhelpful behaviours.

SELF TALK

"Our stories become self-fulfilling; we will always live up to the story. So make it a desired one."
– Malti Bhojwani

All thinking, whether positive or negative, is supported through self-talk. It is the way we interpret our experiences and the messages we give ourselves about them. Choosing your words and thoughts carefully—bringing mindfulness to the table—requires effort, but it is of the utmost importance.

Very often, the internal dialogue we have with ourselves is so harsh that if we said it out loud, we would be shocked! "I'm ugly, I'm overweight, I am inferior compared to my colleagues," and so on. A friend would be hurt if we spoke to them in this manner, as would we if they spoke to us in this way. With this kind of self-talk as a daily diet, no wonder so many of us feel badly about ourselves.

In order to reframe your thinking, one approach is to engage in positive self-talk. It is not necessary to look in the mirror every morning and roar "I am a tiger!", but there are positive affirmations we can make every day that will help us recognize and change our self-talk. Positive affirmations directly counter the negative things we say to ourselves in our heads and change the often damaging core ideas we hold about ourselves.

Here are examples:

"I will not be able to find a job."

Change to:

"I've been able to find new jobs in the past. It make take some time, but I will find one eventually."

"I don't feel confident doing this presentation (course, interview...)."

Change to:

"It is natural to feel nervous doing something new or something I haven't done often, but in the past, I got comfortable with things once I'd done them a few times."

"I feel scared having this difficult conversation with my partner (friend, customer, boss...).

Change to:

"The hardest part is starting the conversation; once we start talking, the nerves subside, and I will feel more comfortable."

Although positive affirmations have always been thought to be useful, there have been some conflicting findings that show that in certain circumstances they can actually be hurtful to positive thinking. For example, people that have low self-esteem and confidence issues may find that making declarations such as "I am beautiful" or "I am lovable" actually cause them more turmoil because it conflicts with what they believe subconsciously. Rather, if affirmations can be phrased as questions, it can open up more of a dialogue and a realistic middle ground instead of setting two extremes between what your subconscious believes and what our conscious is telling it to believe.

This so called interrogative self-talk is more effective than positive affirmations alone, or can be used in conjunction. So, simply asking "am I?" instead of "I am" or "will I?" instead of "I will" can be more constructive in addressing negative self-image issues and encourage those beliefs to become positive.

ELIMINATE HYBRID THINKING

"Shrug off the no's—they are temporary. This is your world.
In your world there is only yes."
– Jolene Stockman

Many people get trapped in a kind of "hybrid thinking"—which is not entirely positive *or* negative. It is a commitment to not wanting something bad, as opposed to wanting something good. For example, rather than thinking "I'd like to have more than enough money", you might think "I don't want to be in debt".

To the brain, there is a distinct difference between how these thoughts are processed. Suffice to say, the brain does not deal with words like "no", "don't", and "not" in a favourable fashion—so it is important to get in the habit of filtering them out of your self-talk.

Remember, you are asking into your life whatever it is you think about so make it positive **and** definite. You will need to begin thinking more about how you wish things to be, rather than dwelling upon how you don't want them to be.

Language and thinking will ultimately dictate how you —positive words will generate good feelings. Make sure to use affirmative statements in your conversations and internal dialogues. Try beginning your sentences with "I want", and never ending them with "but". For lack of a better way of putting it—don't be wishy-washy! Remember that positive thinking is bolstered by a focus on the present so try to eliminate words like "should", "could", and "might" from your vocabulary.

DON'T PERSONALIZE

"Stop letting people who do so little for you control so much
of your mind, feelings and emotions."
– Will Smith

One of the most pervasive types of negative thinking, which often overlays all else, is a propensity to externalize situations and experiences. This means that we make everything about us.

Sometimes we try to couch personalization in positive terms, claiming that we are just sensitive. However, when people perceive you as highly sensitive, they are less likely to be honest with you—giving you feedback which is unreliable in an effort to protect your feelings.

The truth is, personalizing things is a destructive way of thinking that can drive a wedge between you and those around you. Allowing others to affect how we feel about ourselves, leaves us reeling with low self-esteem and causes us to operate in an environment of distrust. In the workplace, personalization is highly unprofessional.

Personalization is a demon, which simply must be tackled. Negative feedback or rejection does not mean that we are incompetent or unlovable. It is important to stop this kind of negative thinking before it gathers momentum.

One way to do this is to practice thought-stopping when personalization arises. Try wearing a rubber band around your wrist, and when you catch yourself getting caught up in this line of thinking, tell yourself to "stop", and snap the band. Practice deep breathing for three or four breaths, and let the thought go.

You may also want to de-sensitize yourself by putting yourself in situations where you know rejection is likely. Being told "no" in both social and work situations is a good way to learn to take care of yourself by cultivating the ability to not personalize.

Key Actions

Consider whether you are someone that tends to have a fixed or growth mindset? Do you avoid challenge or embrace it? Can you think of a recent example where if you'd been more flexible to a challenge that you might have arrived at a different result?

If you think you tend towards a fixed mindset, indentify some steps that you can take towards opening yourself up to growth. Revisit any criticism you may have received recently, even if you previously thought it was unfairly given. Is there anything you can learn from it, no matter how small? Can you find a lesson in it somewhere? Chances are, if you can, that you can help change the meaning of such setbacks or critiques, and become someone that can grow, change, and embrace new challenges without being hung up on past failures—an optimist!

The main cause of feeling stressed or worried are the negative thoughts swirling around in your mind, so you need to get in the habit of challenging them. For each negative thought or difficult situation, think of a response and imagine that you are talking to a friend. Think of one or two positive rebuttals and use them as a way of reminding yourself that there are always two sides to every situation—even though very often we only look at the negative side.

Some people like to set a timer to remind themselves that it's time for some positive self-talk, or you can just use the technique when you're feeling particularly worried or stressed.

Activity

Write down some of your common negative thoughts and create a positive affirmation, or a positive question, with which you could use to replace these thoughts.

4. MINDFULNESS TECHNIQUES

It is very easy to identify our overall patterns of thinking–most of us know if we tend to be generally optimistic or pessimistic–but becoming aware of and changing specific thought patterns is more difficult. This book will provide you with strategies for dealing with negative thinking, but once you put it down, your challenge will be to recognise when you're engaged in this kind of negative thinking.

Most of the time, we are only partially aware of the train of thoughts that is passing through our minds. This is problematic because if the first of these thoughts is a negative one, it can drag a whole string of negative thoughts along behind it–with us along for the ride! Before we know it, we will have embarked on a negative journey of introspection and doom.

The trick is to become aware of our thinking so that we can intercept the first negative thought, and decide what to do with it. So how do we go about this?

The brain processes millions of thoughts per day–and these thoughts are operating consciously and unconsciously to create our own personal reality. Awareness is the precursor to all change–you will need to examine your state of mind and become acquainted with your negative thinking patterns before change is possible.

To get at this kind of understanding, a mindfulness technique can be very useful. Mindfulness techniques include yoga, body scan, and meditation, and there are many classes or online resources, which can help you get started.

The easiest of these techniques is mindfulness meditation. Through a focus on the here and now, mindfulness meditation engages the right side of the brain (as opposed to the analytical left side, which is busy making plans for the future); this, in turn, activates the parasympathetic nervous system, which will result in less stress and better health.

It has been shown that a marked increase in a sense of well-being can occur in just 8 weeks if one commits to practicing this type of meditation for just 10 minutes a day. Amazingly, these changes appear to be long-lasting–they do not result solely from the relaxation achieved during the meditation practice. The psychological benefits, which persist throughout the day, may be a sign that the mind has already begun working to reorganize itself. This aside, you will be well on your way to becoming aware of negative thought patterns, which is our immediate goal.

Mindfulness is a way of paying attention to the present moment in an intentional way. It allows us to become aware of our thoughts and accept them as they are and without judgement. Non-judgement cannot be emphasized enough–when we stop reacting emotionally to our thoughts, their impact on us is diminished.

Liken this to setting your own course in life, rather than being at the mercy of every storm sent your way. Mindfulness allows you to center yourself so that your mood and state will come from within instead of being dictated by external events.

Mindfulness meditation is about being–it is not geared towards making us different. It is designed to help us see ourselves as we are.

Through a mindfulness practice we can regulate our attention and anchor it in the present moment by directing it towards a particular activity, such as breathing, walking, or eating. Whatever practice you choose, it is important to remember that this is not about trying to stop thinking, it is an exercise in observing your thoughts as they are. What follows is an approach that can help you get you started.

SITTING MEDITATION

The Body

1. Choose a time of day when you can readily commit to a daily practice.

2. Choose a quiet spot where you will not be interrupted. Make sure your phone is out of range and the TV is off!

3. Choose your seat. There is no need to sit cross-legged on the floor—you can sit on a chair, if you wish—but there are a few things to keep in mind. Your hips should be higher than your knees, a chair will satisfy this condition, but if you're on the floor, you may need to prop yourself up with a cushion or rolled up towel.

4. Choose loose, comfortable clothing that will not restrict you in any way.

5. Sit with your back straight but not rigid—in other words, relaxed but not slouched—and your hands should rest on your thighs with the palms down.

6. Practice with your eyes open and your gaze resting on the floor in front of you.

Breathing

No specific breathing technique is required for this meditation. Work with whatever comes naturally for you—through your nose, mouth, or some combination of the two. Mindfulness concerns itself with how we find ourselves in the moment, so it's important to just observe the breath and not to try and control it. Just try to become aware of your inhalations and exhalations—you can count them if it helps you.

Thoughts

Take a few minutes to settle into your breathing and then slowly become aware of your thoughts. Remember that this meditation is designed to help you become aware of your thoughts as they are—it is not about trying to stop them.

Most people, especially those new to meditation, notice that their minds are flooded with thoughts. These may consist of everything from the plans which you have for the weekend, the groceries which you have to buy later that day, childhood memories, fantasies, or even a song that is stuck in your head. Buddhists use the term "monkey mind" to describe this kind of rapid, restless, and uncontrollable thinking. You are not alone in this state of mind.

Your job is to simply observe these thoughts and then release them. Let them go. Analyzing them is tantamount to throwing gas on a fire—you don't want to feed them. If you find yourself getting caught up in a thought or a line of thinking, bring yourself back to a focus on the breath. Some people find it useful to say the word "thinking", or another key word to themselves when they observe this happening—this is fine as long as you don't attach a judgement to the event.

Be sure to not to label your thoughts—or any emotion attached to them—as either "good" or "bad". They are what they are, and it is your job to simply become aware of them.

Practice really does make perfect when it comes to mindfulness meditation. It may be simple, but it requires a dedication to regular practice. In order to experience the benefits of your practice, try to commit to 10 minutes for the next 8 weeks. If you find that you can do 10 minutes in the morning and another 10 at night—so much the better!

Once you become aware of your thoughts, you can begin to understand how they contribute to the kind of life you are choosing to create for yourself. Then, you can challenge this line of thinking.

Remember, thoughts and feelings are not facts, and because they are of our own creation, they can be changed.

REST IN A PLACE OF NON-THINKING

"The temple of our purest thoughts is silence."
– Sarah J. Hale

From a neuroplasticity perspective, it is not always possible to minimize negative circuits in the brain simply by creating positive ones. So if you're struggling to switch over to a positive way of thinking, you may want to consider that your negative circuits first need to be turned off. To deactivate unhelpful thought patterns, you may want to neutralize them through a stand-off period of mental silence. Mindfulness meditation is a wonderful example of non-thinking—we are simply observing what is already there. Spend more time in this mental silence before you begin to challenge your thoughts.

PROGRESSIVE MUSCLE RELAXATION

The technique of progressive muscle relaxation teaches you how to monitor and control your muscles with the aim of becoming more relaxed and focused. It is a two-step process starting with the deliberate application of certain muscle groups (e.g., face muscles, leg muscles, and stomach muscles) and then releasing them in turn. Turning your full attention to the process of the tensing and relaxing heightens your awareness to the feeling of tension flowing away, and through repetitive practice, you can learn to recognize when the body is becoming tense. Sometimes our bodies tense up without us even realising it until we turn our attention to it, so by learning to be aware we can stay one step ahead.

Similar to progressive muscle relaxation, a "body scan" is a simple meditative technique to focus your attentions on each part of your body in turn and observe whatever sensations you feel there.

Key actions

Try to set aside 15 minutes each day to practice, and soon you will be tuned in to your body and able to recognize and dissipate stress and tension before it builds up. With a more relaxed body, our minds can be clearer and better under control.

Practice body scan meditation. Lie on your back with your arms relaxed by your sides and eyes closed. Turn your attention to your breathing and notice how your stomach gentles rises and falls with every inhalation and exhalation. Spend 2-3 minutes doing this or longer until you feel relaxed.

Now turn your attention to a small part of your body, such as your right foot. Ask yourself what do you feel there? Warmth, tension, coolness? Try not to analyze what is going on, just make yourself aware of it. Allow your focus to drift slowly up your body from your foot, along your leg all the way up to the crown of your head, and pay attention to every part of your body in turn. Once there, drift back up and down your body again, scanning it and seeing what you learn about all the different sensations held there.

This is an excellent way to get in touch with your body as a whole and unify it. In terms of aiding positive thinking, a body scan is a quick and effective way to reduce stress and increase your ability to focus.

5. FULL-BODIED POSITIVITY

"Think like a man of action, act like a man of thought."
– Henri Bergson

Communicating non-verbally through the way in which you hold yourself and move through life can also be considered positive or negative. Between 60 and 80 percent of communication is non-verbal, consisting of movements and gestures, which often speak louder than words.

Gaining control over body language is an excellent place to begin on the quest for positive thinking. It is a concrete way in which we can begin to take positive action with which our thoughts and feelings can then begin to fall in line.

In the same way that our thoughts and feelings can cause us to slump and feel a little lost, improving our posture and moving with energy can actually change how we feel. This is why going for a run or a long walk will usually make us feel better.

The way in which we carry ourselves and respond physically to those around us is a sub-conscious manifestation of how we feel. Positive movements and gestures communicate such things as enthusiasm, confidence, and interest, whereas negative body language can indicate boredom and low self-esteem.

BODY LANGUAGE / POWER POSES

Social psychologist and researcher Amy Cuddy's research has shown the importance of body posture by revealing that not only do we can change other people's perceptions with our body posture, but we can even change our own body's chemistry. By simply adopting what she calls "power poses" we can increase our levels of testosterone (which helps with stimulation and a sense of well-being) and decrease cortisol (which is associated with stress). Cuddy's research was picked up by much of the mainstream media as it offered quick and practical ways to deal with potentially stressful situations, such as job interviews, and to seize a sense of power.

So what is a power pose? Firstly, there is a difference between high and low power poses. Standing up straight, hands on hips is high power, whereas being slumped over a desk with a curved back is low power. Having folded arms or a stooped head and defensive and submissive or low power poses, and head up arms stretched and legs apart are dominant high power poses.

MENTAL REHEARSAL

Techniques of visualisation and mental rehearsal are well studied in the domain of sports psychology and are shown to positively affect the performance of athletes. By mentally rehearsing the swing of a gold club or a sprint around the athletics track, the athlete uses all of their senses to imagine a future event that has an optimal outcome, focusing on success and on the sensations of being pleased with their performance. World champion golfer Jack Nicklaus is quoted as saying "I never hit a shot, not even in practice, without having a very sharp in-focus picture of it in my head".

But outside of sports psychology, what lessons can we learn from mental rehearsal and can there be everyday applications of these techniques? Can positive imaginary actions create positive outcomes in real life? Some proponents of these techniques suggest that just by visualising scenarios step by step, you can influence your brain and increase the chances of successful outcomes, such as succeeding at work or being recognised for a skill. Learn how to focus on positive imagery and try to mentally visualise in detail the positive outcome you desire and what you have to do to achieve it. Imagery is something we do naturally anyway, after all. When we worry about things, we often flood our mind with negative imagery, such as imagining accidents or embarrassing situations. Visualising is a different skill to general daydreaming, which can just be fantastical or unlikely situations, and in some ways the imagery must have a degree of realism and you must work hard to mentally rehearse it and get all the senses involved.

Although it is hard to gather evidence about the influence of visualisation and positive imagery on everyday situations in our lives, it certainly does have an effect in the world of sports, and it may well have wider applications, even if they are hard to measure.

DON'T FORGET TO SMILE

"Smile in the mirror. Do that every morning and you'll start to see a big difference in your life."
– Yoko Ono

Smiling requires no explanation at all; it means the same thing in every language and every culture. It is also contagious. One of the first things I learned as a young psychologist was that if you smile at someone, they will usually smile right back–How nice!

The next time you're in the coffee shop, try smiling at someone and see what happens. In much the same way your body language can affect how you feel, smiling will feed back into how you feel about yourself and change you for the better.

FEED YOUR BRAIN A HEALTHY DIET

"The mind grows by what it feeds on."
– J.G. Holland

Examine and concern yourself with the external influences that you are exposing your brain to–both consciously and inadvertently.

As much as possible, surround yourself with positive, forward-moving people. Look for things, people, and experiences that make you happy.

1. Watch television programs and read books that will influence your mind in a positive way.

2. Try listening to motivational and personal development speakers. Many people find that while driving or riding to work is a great time for this.

I consciously avoid watching horror movies and negative television. TV soaps may seem innocuous but are by their very nature negative—requiring continuous drama in their storylines, to keep them afloat.

If you like soaps, try this little experiment. Turn the sound off for an episode of your favourite programme and just watch the facial expressions and observe the anger that unfolds. You will be surprised, and maybe even a little shocked!

Key actions

For just 2 minutes a day, try to incorporate some power poses into your routine. The most well-known pose is the "wonder-woman" pose. Stand up straight and tall, stretching your head up to the ceiling and extending to your full height. Puff your chest out and place your hands on your hips. Feel a sense of power flow through you! This simple posture can be universally effective for men and women, young and old, to experience a sense of power and control over themselves and in their environment and can be particularly effective before entering any new or intimidating situations.

Practice some positive mental imagery. Don't just jump to the outcome, but practice each step towards your goal. Also be aware of any worrying you have done recently and pay attention to the negative scenarios you may have imagined in your head. The more aware you are of this, the more you can avoid wasting energy on negative worrying in the future!

6. FORMING NEW POSITIVE HABITS

"Habit is a cable; we weave a thread each day,
and at last we cannot break it."
– Horace Mann

Forming new habits is the root of all successful change. Whatever line of attack you decide to employ on the road to positive thinking, give it a fair chance. New habits take time to form; how long is up for debate and varies from person to person, but assume it will take weeks or months and not days. Research found that it took on average 66 days to form a new habit to the point that it had become an automatic part of their routine (Lally et al, 2010).

A habit is simply a behaviour that has become automatic–one that has been formed and maintained through repetition. Here are some things to consider when developing new, positive behaviours.

1. Prioritize and start small. You can't change everything at once; choose one thing and work on that.

2. Begin with a vision of where you want to end up.

3. Break your task into small, well-defined goals.

By "chaining" habits together we can help build positive habits and reduce negative ones.

IMPLEMENTATION INTENTIONS

How can we bridge the gap between what we want to achieve and make steps towards achieving it? Implementation intentions are strategies that can help us do just that by specifying the "when's" "how's" and "if's" of your behaviour. Known as "if-then" plans, implementation intentions can not only help you achieve goals in the short-term, but also encourage long-term habit formation. For example, you would like to study more so that you achieve better results on an exam. By planning the time and location of study in advance you make it more likely that studying will happen. Once you are in a habit of studying a certain amount of time in your week, it soon assimilates into your routine.

By planning in this way, we help build a lasting framework for positive behaviour and that means we don't just rely on willpower alone to stay on course.

Key actions

Make a plan for how you want to spend your free time for the next month in advance, and think about incorporating positive actions in each day, such as those we have talked about in this book, such as power poses or visualisation techniques. Make realistic goals for the amount of time you can spend on them and the frequency of the exercises. By planning to integrate these positive techniques in your day, this should help the incidence of them occurring, and before you know it, they will become second nature!

7. KEEPING A JOURNAL

"This pouring thoughts out on paper has relieved me.
I feel better and full of confidence and resolution."
– Diet Eman

Journaling is a great way to figure out your thoughts, set goals, and develop plans. By committing these to writing, you will also have a means by which to go back and objectively evaluate your progress. A journal can be a concrete and visual manifestation of positive thinking.

Putting anything in writing reinforces thinking, so be sure that the things you commit to the page have a positive spin—if only to state the action you will need to take in order to change something you don't like. You may want to release negative thoughts onto the page, but always end on a positive note.

As a strategy by which to challenge negative thinking patterns, keeping a "thought journal" is an excellent tool.

THOUGHT JOURNALS

Use the list of cognitive distortions from the last section as a means by which to identify your negative thinking, and use these as the jumping-off point for your Thought Journal. It should look something like this:

1. Identify a situation that you feel unhappy about. Example: "I had a bad interaction with my daughter's teacher."

2. Identify your initial thought. Example: "He must think I'm a horrible parent."

3. Identify what kind of negative thinking this reflects. Example: Self-blaming and polarized thinking.

4. Challenge this way of thinking by re-framing it in a positive light.
    Example: "I learned something here and know I'll handle it differently next time."

A thought journal will help you identify what you need to change, and this will enable you to develop a plan for replacing negative thoughts with positive thinking.

Remember that change is tied to consistent practice. Commit to writing in your journal daily—as a reflective exercise at the same time each day, if you wish, or throughout the day as negative thinking arises.

GRATITUDE JOURNALS

> "Don't cry because it's over, smile because it happened."
> – Dr. Seuss

Keeping a gratitude journal is a wonderful way to actively begin focusing your attention on all that is positive in your life. It really is as simple as writing down things for which you feel grateful, and it is also a great strategy for finishing your day on a positive note. Research by leading psychologist Robert Emmons showed that even after just 3 weeks of keeping a gratitude journal, people reported a host of benefits physically, psychologically, and socially.

Often people who are stuck in a cycle of negativity have trouble coming up with material for this kind of journal. The trick is to start small—no matter how grim things look, there is always something to be grateful for. Start with food, clothing, and shelter and build out from there. A stranger smiled at you, someone held a door open—you get the picture!

Be careful not to let the number of things you have to write or the time of day you have to do it become obstacles to this process. The most important thing with any journaling is to do it regularly so that it becomes a habit.

CONCLUSION

POSITIVE THINKING AND REALITY

> "I love those who can smile in trouble..."
> – Leonardo da Vinci

Positive thinking is not intended to shield us from reality. It is important to see things the way they are, while acknowledging that we are in charge of the story that we choose to tell ourselves.

Life is full of challenges, the key is being able to frame and deal with them in a positive manner. Try to see negative events as planting the seeds of change which will take you to a better place, and use them as motivation to move you forward.

Often, the most challenging times provide the most valuable learning experiences in life. Optimists are great problem solvers–they believe in their abilities and expect to succeed. When things don't work out the way they planned, they quickly pick up the pieces and move on.

A healthy approach to embracing the negative bears the following in mind:

1. All setbacks are temporary.

2. There is a lesson to be learned in every experience: what has it taught you, how can it make you a better person, or move you in the direction of the vision you have for yourself?

3. Don't dwell on the negative details of the experience. Analyzing is not essential to change–rumination interferes with problem solving and leads to avoidance rather than action.

4. Don't personalize—try to imagine yourself as a "fly-on-the-wall" in order to distance yourself emotionally from negative experiences. A bad experience does not make you a bad person. Not everything has to feel good, but remember, feelings are not facts. Try to observe the situation in much in the same way you observe your thoughts in the mindfulness meditation—objectively and without judgment.

5. Draw up a plan for QUICKLY moving forward. Convert mistakes into knowledge. Accept responsibility for your choices, factor the result into your next decision, and move on.

WHAT TO TAKE AWAY FROM THIS

"Every dream begins with a dreamer. Always remember, you have within you the strength, the patience, and the passion to reach for the stars to change the world." – Harriet Tubman

In your quest to switch out negative thinking for positive, remember that you are trying to improve the quality of your life by reclaiming control over it. You will do this by formulating a vision of how you want your life to look and by moving patiently towards it

As you embark on this life changing journey, remember that all change takes time. The key to your success lies in applying self-discipline and perseverance to the practice of the techniques described in this book.

At all costs, don't personalize things. If something doesn't work out the way you planned, avoid internalizing it as an indication that you are not capable or are unworthy of great things. Instead, learn from it and move on—reminding yourself of all that is positive about you and your life.

REFERENCES

Seligman, Martin E.P. 1991. *Learned Optimism: How to Change Your Mind and Your Life.* New York: A. A. Knopf.

Dweck, C. S. 2006. *Mindset: The New Psychology of Success.* New York: Random House.

Reivich, K, and A. Shatté. 2002. The Resilience Factor: 7 Keys to Finding Your Inner Strength and Overcoming Life's Hurdles. New York: Broadway Books.

Maymin, S. 2007. *The A.P.E. Method to Get Out of A Bad Mood.* http://positivepsychologynews.com/news/senia-maymin/20070601270

Bandler, R. and J. Grinder. 1981. *Frogs into Princes: Neuro Linguistic Programming.* United States: Real People Press.

Carney, Dana R., A. J. Cuddy and A. J. Yap. 2010. Power Posing – Brief Nonverbal Displays Affect Neuroendocrine Levels and Risk Tolerance. *Journal of the Association for Psychological Science* 21 (10): 1363–1368.

Lally, P., C. H. van Jaarsveld, H.W. W. Potts, and J. Wardle. 2010. How are habits formed: Modelling habit formation in the real world. *European Journal of Social Psychology* 40 (6): 998–1009.

Emmons, R. 2008. *Thanks!: How Practicing Gratitude Can Make You Happier.* New York: Mariner Books.

Printed in Great Britain
by Amazon